DDD

Prism
Series
Volume 4

How to Use Differentiated Instruction

With Developmental Disabilities in the General Education Classroom

by Barbara C. Gartin, Nikki L. Murdick,
Marcia Imbeau, and Darlene E. Perner

Council for
Exceptional
Children

A Publication of the
Division on Developmental Disabilities
of the Council for Exceptional Children

HOW TO USE DIFFERENTIATED INSTRUCTION WITH STUDENTS WITH DEVELOPMENTAL DISABILITIES IN THE GENERAL EDUCATION CLASSROOM

FOREWORD

Our nation's history is built on two key values-equity and excellence. In education, our equity heritage leads us to believe that all of our young citizens deserve access to a high quality education that prepares them to participate fully and vigorously in a dynamic society. Our excellence focus guides us to the premise that all our young citizens should have the chance to become the best person they can be.

Those are ambitious values in the best of settings. In contemporary classrooms, they are devilishly difficult to achieve.

Even cities and towns where immigration has previously been an academic concept now have large populations of students for whom English is a second language. Varied cultures shape students variously even when language is not an issue. In virtually every school, sizeable numbers of students grapple with physical, cognitive, and/or behavioral challenges. In the same schools are students who spend most of their school careers waiting for challenge because they come to school years ahead of prescribed curricula.

There are, of course, also more "typical" students-those for whom the timelines, learning sequences, and materials of school are designed. Even these students learn in varied ways and represent the widest possible range of interests and dreams. Add to that mix students whose home lives are so dark that they threaten to extinguish all light from the young they are charged to protect. Of course, many students represent several of these categories at once—a child who cannot see, but who excels in mathematics—a learner who speaks no English and has a learning disability—a student who is a brilliant writer, terrified to go home at the end of the day, and who has a behavioral disorder.

In such classrooms, teachers are generally provided one textbook for all comers. The school class, day, and year are standard lengths, despite the non-standard student population. Grading systems do more to reinforce the obvious than to support maximum growth in all students. Now, teachers are also faced with lists of learning goals that are often long, fragmented, and decontextualized, and with what appear to be political mandates to ensure that all students arrive at a normative point of understanding by a specified calendar date and that each student be ready to express that understanding in an identical format.

Teaching has never been more challenging. Yet great challenges always carry with them great opportunity.

We are situated at a moment in our national educational history when we have the opportunity to learn anew how to craft classrooms in which each student has access to high quality knowledge, understanding, and skill. There are three significant implications contained in this opportunity. First, we can no longer accept classrooms that relegate some students to low level learning. Second, in addition to providing rich, powerful, high quality curriculum for all learners, we must ensure instructional support systems that make it possible for each learner to take advantage of what a high quality curriculum has to offer. Third, we must learn how to establish the goal of ensuring that each student grows as much as he or she can grow at a given time—and how to acknowledge the growth appropriately when it occurs.

To succeed in establishing classrooms where all students work with ideas and skills that equip them for a future of continued learning, to provide support systems that promote systematic development of the individual, and to settle for nothing less than the best a student has to offer is to achieve classrooms that represent both equity and excellence. What a challenge! What an opportunity!

In this book, four educators who know both the scholarship and practice of education have collaborated to move forward the educational conversation about how to achieve classrooms that prepare in advance to give students maximum opportunity and expect maximum growth—and to extend a teacher's repertoire for doing so. Barbara Gartin, Nikki Murdick, Marcia Imbeau, and Darlene Perner provide frameworks for planning learning environments, content, process, and products that enable students with learning challenges to succeed with meaningful curriculum. They offer decision-making guidelines for teachers who must work with standardized curriculum and non-standardized students.

In addition, the book gives concrete, detailed examples of how the curricular and instructional frameworks would look when applied to the learning needs of students with a range of learning needs and in a range of grade levels and subjects. Up-to-date web sites provide a wealth of resources for educators who continue to seek insights about classrooms that genuinely work for all young people who count on them. The authors also wisely caution us to include in our plans for differentiation the collection of data to assess our successes and guide our future work.

This book is, in my opinion, an example of "defensible" differentiation. It is not a bag of instructional tricks to be used randomly in the classroom. Rather, it offers a sound rationale for beginning with quality curriculum and then making purposeful classroom modifications to support success of students who have difficulty accessing, remembering, or expressing the ideas, skills, and understandings that help young people become effective learners and contributors.

Carol Ann Tomlinson, Ed.D.

Professor of Educational Leadership, Foundations, and Policy

The University of Virginia

ACKNOWLEDGEMENTS

Starting during our student years and continuing into our professional lives, the Council for Exceptional Children has been a constant source of professional support. This book is our attempt to thank the organization in a small way for the tremendous assistance that CEC and the Division on Developmental Disabilities has provided throughout the years.

There are also several individuals we would like to thank. First, we thank Carol Ann Tomlinson for translating Jean Maker's ideas into the language of teachers. Secondly, we thank Tom E.C. Smith and the other officers of the Division on Developmental Disabilities for allowing us to share our thoughts on Differentiation of Instruction through this PRISM book. Finally, we thank our reviewers, Kim Carper and Ed Polloway, our editor, Jack Hourcade, and Phil Parette, consulting editor, for their invaluable suggestions and work.

C H A P T E R

1

PHILOSOPHICAL OVERVIEW

Today's schools house a student body that is culturally, economically, and linguistically diverse with disparate needs and abilities. As diversity increases, grouping students by such factors as readiness or ability becomes an increasingly questionable practice. Diversities that must be addressed in today's schools include not only the issues of student readiness, language and culture, and ability/disability, but also student interests and individual learning profiles. Today's educational professionals are seeking a means of addressing the issue of diversity in the classroom through the use of appropriate teaching strategies.

> Given the increasingly diverse student population schools today are challenged to serve, we should not still be asking whether it is feasible to provide for student diversity in heterogeneous classes. The question at hand is how we can best respond to student diversity so that outcome standards are upheld for every student, including the most difficult to teach and most challenging to motivate ("Issue", 1994, p. 7).

Two developments in education seek to address this challenge. The first is the philosophy of inclusion. The second is the growth of the use of differentiated instruction.

What is Inclusion?

When the term "inclusion" appears, many people think of mainstreaming and individualized instruction. But inclusion is a philosophy, not a teaching methodology. According to Shea and Bauer (1997), inclusion supports the belief that all students, regardless of ability, are a vital and integral part of the general education system. Inclusion reflects the beliefs that all children should be taught in neighborhood schools and that instruction can and should be designed to meet the needs of students within their classroom.

The basic components of the philosophy of inclusion include the following:

- emphasis on neighborhood schools

- equitable assignment of students in general education classrooms throughout the school district

- provision of educational services without regard to disability type or severity

- placement according to appropriate age and grade

- usage of supportive forms of instruction in the general education classroom including peer instruction and cooperative learning

- provision of special education supports in an integrated general education environment (Janney & Snell, 2000; Shea & Bauer, 1997).

Increasingly inclusion is being seen as a means of addressing the needs of the diverse, multicultural student body in schools today. One of the significant challenges to inclusive programs is the question of how to meet the diverse educational needs of students in a way that is efficient and effective. This is especially true when educating children who are different, whether that difference is one of abilities, or language and ethnic background. The varying needs of children often do not lend themselves to the "whole-class" method of teaching. The alternative one-to-one method of individualization may be neither feasible nor advisable. Differentiated instruction, however, has shown considerable promise as a method for addressing the issue of including all students in general education classes.

What is Differentiated Instruction?

Differentiated instruction is defined here as the planning of curriculum and instruction using strategies that address student strengths, interests, skills, and readiness in flexible learning environments. Tomlinson (2000a) went on to suggest that differentiated instruction is "a way of thinking about teaching and learning" (p. 6). It is an approach to education that holds that:

- students differ in their readiness to learn;

- students differ in their readiness significantly enough to impact their learning;

- students learn best with high expectations and support from adults;

- students learn best when material is connected to their interests and experiences;

- students learn best in a safe community; and

- schools must maximize each student's capacity.

These beliefs serve as guiding principles to direct the actions of teachers.

In 1995, Carol Ann Tomlinson provided a precise description of what differentiated instruction is and is not (see Table 1.1).

Table 1.1   What Differentiated Instruction Is and Is Not

> ✍ Differentiated instruction is used to reach the goal set for student learning <u>not</u> instruction based on fragmented student skill stages.
>
> ✍ Differentiated instruction uses ever-changing grouping for learning, <u>not</u> static homogeneous groups.
>
> ✍ Differentiated instruction is based on well-planned lessons directed toward the instructional goal, <u>not</u> activity-based, chaotic instruction.
>
> ✍ Differentiated instruction includes clarifying the depth and nature of the content, <u>not</u> adjusting the content by adding more or requiring less.
>
> ✍ Differentiated instruction accepts student products based on individual characteristics, <u>not</u> products based on teacher choice.
>
> Tomlinson, 1995.

She stated that it was not the "individualized instruction" of the 1970s where the teacher attempted to develop, implement, and evaluate instructional programs for each member of an entire class of students. That form of individualizing instruction resulted in numerous "mini" classrooms instead of a single classroom learning community. As this form of instruction required the teacher to manage 25 to 30 different instructions per subject per class, it was doomed to failure.

An outgrowth of this failed concept was the fear that differentiated instruction will be chaotic and teachers will not be in control of the learning environment. However, a teacher developing differentiated instructional plans needs more, not less, control. If a differentiated classroom is to be effective, then pre-planning of the lessons with focused goals, objectives, materials, resources, and assessment plans is essential.

There is also a concern that the use of grouping in attempting to differentiate instruction will lead to a reemergence of academic tracking. However, grouping within a differentiated classroom is flexible and dynamic, not fixed. Group membership is based on multiple factors including interest, aptitude, readiness, and previous knowledge. Group membership may change as the instructional variables change.

An additional concern is that the use of grouping may merely change student requirements so that some "do more" and others "do less". In other words, differentiation is based on the group in which the student is placed. In this scenario, students who need a more advanced lesson "do more" of the same work. For example, these students receive lesson assignments and activities that are not more difficult or complex but just more of the same as initially required. Students for whom the original assignment is too difficult do not receive an activity that has been modified according to their present skill level. They just "do less" of the same work. In contrast, differentiated instruction results in a lesson designed to address the specified instructional goal using strategies that incorporate student strengths and present skill levels. This form of differentiation of instruction should result in student success.

One difficulty that sometimes arises is that teachers see differentiated instruction as a means of lesson planning, not as a method for developing curriculum for successful learning and instruction. The focus on lessons without an overarching plan can result in a disjointed curriculum. In order to address this difficulty, Tomlinson (2000b) proposed a line of logic that will lead to successful differentiation of curriculum for all students (see Table 1.2). This line of logic emphasizes a solid, high quality curriculum as the essential component of any effective differentiated instruction plan. This curriculum would include content that is concept and generalization-based, has high relevance, is coherent and transferable, and is powerful and authentic (Tomlinson, 2000b). In developing curriculum for most students with developmental disabilities, teachers must consider the goal of access to the general education curriculum for all students. The use of integrated differentiated curricula in the inclusive classroom can supply the teacher with a critical element in the effective instructional planning process for inclusive education.

Table 1.2   Line of Logic for Differentiation

> ✐ Learners differ.
>
> ✐ Learning requires challenge, success, connection, fit.
>
> ✐ Challenge, success, connection, and fit do not occur by ignoring student differences.
>
> ✐ A flexible approach to teaching is essential.
>
> ✐ Successful attention to student differences must be rooted in solid curriculum.
>
> ✐ Effective attention to student differences must be rooted in an environment of mutual respect, safety, emphasis on individual growth, and shared responsibility for learning.
>
> ✐ Principles of effective differentiation stem from and exist to ensure high quality curriculum, maximum individual growth, and sense of community.
>
> ✐ There are many routes to achieving high quality curriculum taught in ways that attend to student differences and build community.
>
> Tomlinson, 2000b, p. 6.

Summary

Challenges inherent in the inclusive, diverse classrooms of today can be met through the concept of differentiated instruction. Early application of differentiated instruction activities focused on children who were gifted and talented and on students with differing learning profiles. More recent application has used differentiated instruction strategies within the inclusive classroom to enhance the effectiveness of instruction for students with learning and behavioral disabilities. With the search for strategies to enhance the curricula for an increasingly diverse student body, differentiated instruction has become the "catch word" for curricular development for all students in general education classrooms. Students with varying academic readiness, interest levels, and individual learning profiles including those with severe learning and behavioral disabilities are now being included in general education classrooms. For their teachers who have often not received an in-depth preparation in classroom modifications for students with this diversity of needs, this monograph will provide a starting point for preparing curricula and lessons that incorporate instructional differentiation.

CHAPTER

2

A MODEL FOR DIFFERENTIATING INSTRUCTION IN THE INCLUSIVE CLASSROOM

In order to effectively differentiate instruction, it is essential to discuss the concept of curriculum and how, or if, it differs from the concept of instruction. Two views of curriculum are described. According to Mercer and Mercer (2001), "curriculum primarily involves what is taught in the school and consists of learning outcomes that society considers essential for success" (p. 170). Meyen (1981) on the other hand describes curriculum quite differently:

The term *curriculum* is frequently and varyingly defined as the courses offered, the overall experience provided a child by the school, the program included in a particular subject field, or in some cases, the sum total of experiences afforded school-age children regardless of school sponsorship. (pp. 20-21)

When educators are faced with the issue of developing and implementing instruction for students with varying abilities, this question of curriculum becomes especially significant. Hoover and Patton (1997) considered the issue of curriculum to be "one of the first issues classroom teachers encounter in the overall teaching and learning process" (p. 6). Without having a clear understanding of what constitutes a curriculum and the forms in which it appears it is often impossible for teachers to adequately design instruction that is effectively differentiated.

Types of Curricula

Curricula can be identified as one of three types: (a) explicit, (b) hidden, or (c) absent (Hoover & Patton, 1997). An explicit curricula can be defined as the formal curriculum developed by the district through its stated policy development process. This is the curriculum with which teachers are the most familiar, but perhaps is also the one that is the least followed when classroom instruction is designed.

The *hidden curriculum* is the one that the teachers actually teach. According to Hoover and Patton (1997), the hidden curriculum is developed "as teachers make inferences about the explicit curriculum they are required to teach" (p. 7).

The final type of curriculum is called the absent curriculum. As teachers and schools select the content of the explicit and hidden curriculum, a number of topics are omitted. These make up the absent curriculum. Unfortunately, those omitted topics may be just as important as what is actually taught.

As Tomlinson and Allan (2000) stated, difficulty may arise when teachers begin to plan for differentiated instruction within their classroom. This difficulty is often aggravated as: "...teachers sometimes find themselves struggling against a district curriculum that seems more standardized than differentiated. This situation is aggravated if the curriculum is largely a collection of topics, facts, and skills-a difficult kind of curriculum to differentiate (pp. 90-91)."

What Is the Relationship Between Curriculum and Instruction?

In today's classrooms, teachers are required to design instruction not only to meet the specific, instructional needs of students, but to meet the curriculum standards set forth by state and federal mandate. Designing effective instruction requires an answer to three basic questions:

1. What is the terminal goal of the instructional path?

2. How do you plan to get to the terminal goal?

3. How will you know when you have reached the goal?

As the teacher creates instructional plans for the students in the classroom, these three questions must be considered. As Tomlinson (1999) noted, "hazy" lessons do not support differentiated instruction. This is because:

> when a teacher lacks clarity about what a student should know, understand, and be able to do as a result of a lesson, the learning tasks she creates may or may not be engaging and we can almost be certain the tasks won't help students understand essential ideas or principles. A fuzzy sense of the essentials results in fuzzy activities,

which, in turn, results in fuzzy student understanding. (p. 37)

The remedy is to plan a focused curriculum with a clear idea of the relationship between curriculum and instruction (Tomlinson, 2001). A focused curriculum articulates distinct goals concerning what students should know (e.g., facts, vocabulary), understand (e.g., concepts, principles or generalizations) and be able to do (e.g., skills) as a result of the lesson, lesson sequence, unit, and year of instruction. From this information, one should be able to prepare instruction that (a) is of high quality, and (b) addresses the key principles of a differentiated classroom. Tomlinson (1999) suggested that high quality instruction:

- is focused on essential understandings/skills

- is engaging to the student

- is joyful or satisfying

- provides choices

- has clear expectations

- allows meaningful collaboration

- is focused on products that matter to the student

- connects with the student's lives and world

- is fresh and surprising

- seems real or is real to the student

- is coherent to the student (organized, unified, sensible)

- is rich, deals with profound ideas

- stretches the student

- leads the student to use learning in interesting/important ways

- involves the student in setting learning goals and assessing progress

Similarly, Tomlinson (1999) proposed that in a differentiated classroom:

- The teacher is clear in what matters about the subject matter.

- The teacher understands, appreciates and builds upon student differences.

- Assessment and instruction are inseparable.

- The teacher adjusts content, process, and product in response to student readiness, interests, and learning profile.

- All students participate in respectful work.

- Students and teachers are collaborators in learning.

- Educational goals are maximum growth and individual success.

- Flexibility is the hallmark of a differentiated classroom.

The Essential Elements of Differentiation

In order to incorporate the principles of a differentiated instruction and prepare a curriculum that is of high quality, the teacher must understand that the curriculum can be divided into three specific and interrelated components: (a) content, (b) process, and (c) product (Tomlinson, 1995). Each of these is varied in anticipation of and response to student differences in readiness, interest, and learning needs. According to Maker (1993) and Janney and Snell (2000), an additional component that must be considered when planning a differentiated classroom is that of learning environment. These four components are further described as follows.

Content

The content can be defined as what the student should know or understand and as a result of this learning be able to do. In other words this is what will be taught, and is determined by the teacher, school, district and/or state standards.

Process

The process refers to the activities, lessons, and interactions that occur during the school day to help the student make sense of the content being presented. They are the structure that supports the content.

Product

Products are the result of the "sense-making activities" (or process), and may be used as an assessment instrument to assure the student has learned the desired curriculum. In other words, they are the means by which the student demonstrates successful acquisition of knowledge.

Learning Environment

The learning environment includes all facets of the classroom and school; in other words, where the learning is to occur. Thus a review of the learning environment would take into consideration the physical outlook and plan of the classroom as well as the school, the number and type of grouping of the students within the classroom, and the physical environment such as heat, light, and noise. Each of these factors will impact either positively or negatively on any curriculum and instruction.

Each of these elements is interrelated with the others. The teacher who is planning to differentiate classroom curriculum and instruction for students with varying abilities must consider each of the components. To assist in this process, Tomlinson and Allan (2000) developed their "Guide for Planning Differentiated Instruction" which uses a question format to support the instructional planner in the planning process. That guide includes the following:

1. Are you clear on what you want the student to know (facts, information), understand (principles, generalizations, ideas) and be able to do as a result of this/these learning experience(s)?

2. In deciding on content, have you thought about and selected alternate sources and resources, varied support systems, and/or varied pacing plans?

3. Have you made plans to pre-assess student readiness so you can prepare appropriate content and/or activity?

4. As you assign students to groups or tasks, have you made certain groups vary from previous recent ones, students are encouraged to "work up", provisions are made (if appropriate) for students who need or prefer to work alone, and/or group-size matches student need?

5. As you created differentiated activities, have you made certain that:

   a. all of them call for high-level thinking

   b. all of them appear about equally interesting to your learners

c. they vary along the continuum of the equalizer

d. students have choices to make about how to apply skills or how to express them

e. opportunities for varied modes of learning are provided

f. each activity is squarely focused on one (or a few) key concepts and generalizations

g. student choice is provided

h. appropriate skills have been integrated into activity requirements

i. expectations are clearly delineated

j. a plan for gathering ongoing assessment has been developed

k. and a plan/mechanism for bringing closure and clarity has been identified?

6. When creating assignments for differentiated products, have you made certain that they:

a. vary along the continuum based on student readiness

b. require all students to use key concepts, generalizations, ideas to solve problems and create meaningful products

c. provide student choice

d. provide delineated and appropriately challenging expectations for content of the product

e. provide for additional criteria for success to be added by student and teacher

f. provide plans for formative and summative evaluation

g. have parent involvement as appropriate?

7. Have you also thought about the use of various instructional strategies (contracts, centers, compacting, etc.), the use of small groups for instruction, student sampling for understanding, development of meaningful tasks for reinforcement, extension, and exploration? (Tomlinson & Allan, 2000, pp. 142-143.)

Critical Factors in Implementing an Instructional Planning Model

Before one can implement any model of instructional planning, there are a number of essential features that must be discussed with the school administration. The following elements must be considered and plans developed to address each for successful implementation of the differentiated instruction model to occur.

First, the essentials of the plan must be considered.

- Who will prepare the plan?

- Who will implement it?

- Are these the same people?

Differentiated instruction often requires time to locate or prepare materials and funding to cover the cost.

- Who will pay?

- Where will materials be stored and who has custody of them?

- Who will monitor and evaluate the actions taken toward the implementation of the program?

- What are the criteria for success?

Answers to such questions must be addressed, and possibly negotiated with the school administration. This needs to be done prior to implementation with all involved parties receiving the information.

Second, after all parties have approved the plan, the actual work begins. Identification of student and class needs must occur. Data need to be collected to determine whether individual students have difficulty (a) accessing the content, (b) storing or remembering the content, or (c) expressing or demonstrating competency. Identification of learner profiles must also occur. The question then arises of who will perform the assessment and how.

One concern that is often posed when differentiated instruction is being considered is whether modification is the most appropriate way for students to be successful. The implementation of differentiated instruction does not supersede the provision of intensive instruction in academic and social domains.

A related concern for students with developmental disabilities is whether the location of the instruction is in the general education classroom or in a more specialized setting. The preferred setting for instruction of *all* students is the general education classroom. This preference is supported in the 1997 IDEA Amendments that cited the general education classroom and curriculum as the focal point for the instruction of students with disabilities. However, decisions concerning the most appropriate educational setting for a student ultimately must be based on that student's unique and specific needs.

Finally, it is imperative that anyone who uses a model for differentiated instruction consider the issue of short-term adaptations versus life-long skill development. The focus of an effective educational plan is to provide students with skills leading to success in the future. Adaptations through a differentiated instruction curricular model support that goal. Those developing a plan for students with diverse needs must assure that incompetence or dependency is not built into the plan through the instructional adaptations.

Developing an Effective Planning Model

A model that lends itself to successful inclusion is that of Schumm, Vaughn, and Leavell's (1994) "Planning Pyramid" (see Figure 2.1). This model provides a framework for planning for diverse students' needs, and focuses on the identification of adaptations as a component of any comprehensive plan developed for students with mild disabilities.

Table 2.1   The Planning Pyramid

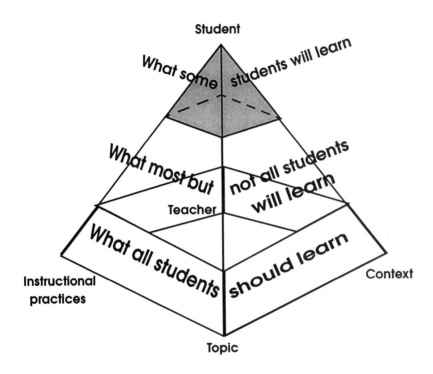

Schumm et al. (1994) suggested that teachers should plan some of the adaptations prior to lesson planning by first reflecting on the five "points of entry":

- the topic,

- the students,

- the classroom context,

- the teacher, and

- the appropriate instructional practices.

After reflection they should then determine what is to be taught and how. Following that teachers then should identify the specific instructional practices and requisite adaptations in order to assure that learning occurs for all students (see Schumm, 1999 for a more in-depth description of steps in using the Planning Pyramid). Although this model is designed for use in content area instruction, it can be utilized in designing differentiated lessons in the inclusive, diverse classrooms of today.

The Planning Pyramid Model

Schumm et al. (1994) developed the Planning Pyramid as a means of assisting teachers in the adaptation of content area textbooks. Their work is invaluable to teachers working with students who are learning material at different speeds, who are functioning at different academic levels, who have varying levels of academic readiness, who have diverse learning preferences, and who have a wide range of interests.

The Planning Pyramid (see Figure 2.1) has two primary dimensions: the five "points" of the pyramid (four at the base and one at the top), and the three vertical levels or tiers. The base of the pyramid has four points:

- topic

- classroom context

- teacher

- appropriate instructional practices.

The apex of the pyramid, the fifth factor, is the student. When the teacher begins the planning process and uses the Planning Pyramid, these five points of entry, or mitigating factors, serve as reflection keys. Before any planning can occur the teacher should understand each factor and its impact(s) within the learning environment.

The second dimension of the pyramid is its vertical division into three tiers that correspond to degrees of learning. The base or lower tier consists of "What *all* students will learn". The middle tier is "What *most* but not all students will learn", while the top tier is "What *some* students will learn". Using the information developed during reflection and the three tiers of the pyramid, objectives for each level can be designed. The information can then be compiled on the The Instructional Planning Form (see Figure 2.2).

Table 2.2   Instructional Planning Form

Date: _____   Period: _____   Subject: _____

Goal: _____

Materials Required: _____

	Anticipatory Set	Learning Activity	Rehearsal Activity	Learning Activity	Evaluation Activity
What some will learn:					
What most will learn:					
What all should learn (Goal):					
Adaptations •Content •Product •Process •Environment					

Once the objective(s) are developed and the content defined for each of the pyramid levels, then the teacher can list adaptations. The majority of intensive adaptations will occur at the base tier, as this is the level where all students must learn the information. Teachers who use this format can clearly note the essential facets of the lesson. But in order to assure that students with learning and behavioral needs are not relegated to the base tier throughout their school career, modifications must also be presented that would assist them in reaching the middle and/or the top tier of the pyramid.

According to Schumm (1999), the Planning Pyramid can be used for individual lessons, weekly lessons, or even unit plans or theme cycles. This structure provides teachers with a planning format, as well as a means of communicating with parents and other professionals about student instructional goals in comparison with others in the class. Figure 2.2, the Instructional Planning Form, shows how a teacher can develop a planning form incorporating the components of the Planning Pyramid.

Curricula for the Inclusive Classroom

Curriculum typically is established long before the students enter the school. A curriculum represents what society values as important for becoming a productive citizen and successful individual. Information about possible curricula can be obtained from commercial curriculum guides, district frameworks, state standards, and literature from learned societies.

If the curriculum accurately represents what is important knowledge within society, then it should have the potential to provide all students the opportunity to acquire this "important" knowledge and skills. However, to accommodate students with diverse needs, it may be necessary to prioritize the content to ensure that the most important content is mastered (What all need to know). Teachers should teach so that all students obtain an understanding and mastery of this most critical content.

After determining what all students should know, content must be organized and sequenced. Unit objectives must be determined. Instructional objective(s) must be defined. A task analysis of the concept being taught might be helpful. In that task analysis, the content of the lesson is broken down into several smaller, simpler, and easier to learn tasks.

Then the teacher selects exemplars and nonexemplars. The selection of books, materials, and additional resources should include a wide array of reading levels, interests, and input modalities. Presentations, evaluations, and activities must be planned. Diverse teaching materials must be obtained or developed. These decisions provide the framework for structuring instruction. The richer the resources available to the teacher, the greater the possibility of meeting the diverse needs of the students within the inclusive classroom. In the next four chapters, the four critical elements of differentiation (learning environment, content, process, and product) will be discussed to better prepare teachers who are implementing differentiated instruction for their students with developmental disabilities within the inclusive classroom.

Summary

When the decision to implement differentiated instruction in a diverse classroom is made, perhaps the first issue that must be addressed is the curriculum. Without a clear understanding of the district's explicit standardized curriculum and how it differs from the hidden curriculum (that is, what is actually taught in the classroom), it becomes difficult to adequately design differentiated lessons for successful learning.

Tomlinson (1995, 1999, 2001) suggested that curricula can be divided into the specific components of content, process, product, and learning environment. The teacher involved in developing a differentiated instructional plan should address each of these in that process. Although these components may be addressed individually, they are fundamentally interrelated.

The Planning Pyramid (Schumm, Vaughan, & Leavell, 1994) provides an effective structure to incorporate these components when planning for differentiated instruction. In the next four chapters, the specific elements of differentiated instruction (learning environment, content, process, and product) will be reviewed to better prepare the teacher of diverse students, including those with developmental disabilities, in inclusive classrooms.

3

LEARNING ENVIRONMENT CONSIDERATIONS

Creating a learning environment that fosters respect, encouragement, acceptance and joy is the goal of every inclusive classroom. A learning environment such as this would emphasize that all students are respected and that all student work is important and valued.

Every teacher is responsible for setting the tone of the classroom. His/her attitudes, enthusiasm and expectations influence the feelings and perceptions of students concerning themselves and others. This chapter will explore the characteristics of a healthy inclusive classroom, and will share examples of how a teacher might design the classroom environment to support learning for all.

How Does a Teacher Develop a Healthy Learning Environment?

Implementing a philosophy of inclusion and differentiation requires that teachers implement "significant changes in curricular and instructional practices, and in teacher roles and responsibilities" (Janney & Snell, 2000, p. 197), along with changes in the physical environment of the classroom. The three major areas of healthy learning environments that will be discussed in this chapter are (a) classroom physical arrangements, (b) instructional groupings, and (c) classroom climates. Each of these areas will be described, with specific implications for use in classrooms with students with developmental disabilities identified.

Classroom Physical Arrangement

Teachers might begin with a review and preparation of the physical space in which the community of learners will work and play every day. When assessing the physical environment, the teacher should consider such aspects of the classroom as access to others; adequacy of space; mobility issues in the room and building; distraction-free or reduced distraction areas; and access to manipulative materials, and to technology (see Table

3.1 for an expanded learning environment checklist). These decisions are especially important in an inclusive classroom incorporating differentiated instruction. Creating a climate where everyone has access to the teacher and the materials is necessary for student success.

Table 3.1   Learning Environment Checklist

Seating allows for:

- ✐ quiet places (study carrels, loner seats, reading corners, headphone area, conference area)
- ✐ flexible seating arrangements and grouping
- ✐ multiple use areas (group work area, tutorial stations, workstation area with easy access to materials)

Classroom Organization includes:

- ✐ well-established daily routines
- ✐ clear rules with consistent enforcement
- ✐ multiple signals and cues to prepare students for changes in activity
- ✐ student assignments given orally, posted on the board and written in assignment workbooks
- ✐ manipulatives and materials stored for easy access as needed
- ✐ easy access storage for wheelchair or crutches
- ✐ aisles that allow students easy movement around the classroom
- ✐ uncluttered classrooms

Positive climate practices established by the teacher include:

- ✐ well established behavioral expectations that have been taught and reinforced regularly
- ✐ prevention of difficulties through teaching appropriate behaviors
- ✐ posted reminders that are used in praise and correction
- ✐ use of physical proximity and touch to help student refocus
- ✐ reduction or elimination of textures, sounds and smells that might be disconcerting to some learners
- ✐ individual positive attention to each student that promotes actions that tell the student that he or she is valued, able, and trusted
- ✐ development of independent thought and action in each student
- ✐ acceptance and valuing of diversity in people and thought
- ✐ love and joy in teaching and learning

How can the classroom physical arrangement be modified to support learning for students with developmental disabilities? According to Janney and Snell (2000), one way is to modify the place where instruction occurs. Two examples provided by Janney and Snell (2000) are (a) provision of privacy through the addition of a study carrel or a private office within the classroom, and (b) strategic placement of individual student desks to support learning (e.g., out of high-traffic areas, away from particular peers, near the teacher's desk, near the chalkboard) (p. 22).

Additional modifications of the classroom environment include flexible scheduling and programming, and a room arrangement that is flexible enough to employ a variety of different instructional arrangements (Bartlett, Weisenstein, & Etscheidt, 2002; Bos & Vaughn, 2002). Whatever the type of instructional arrangement, it should be remembered that its goal is to assist in addressing the varying learning needs of the students in the classroom.

Miller (2002) identified two aspects of the physical dimension that contribute to student learning and behavior: (a) seating arrangements, and (b) special activity areas such as computer stations, free time areas, and learning centers. The arrangement of students' desks should be determined by the types of activities and amount of independence that will be expected of the students. Students with developmental disabilities may need desks positioned away from distracters such as doors and windows, or in quieter areas of the classroom for independent work. But "this positioning should not...result in the student feeling isolated or separated from the other students in the room" (Miller, 2002, p. 120) or the goal of a positive classroom climate will be lost.

Instructional Grouping

Arranging the environment through the use of flexible grouping can assist students in learning (Bos & Vaughn, 2002). Instructional grouping arrangements include large-group instruction, small-group instruction, one-to-one instruction, independent learning activities, cooperative learning groups, and peer teaching pairs. When planning for classes in which students with developmental disabilities are included, the teacher should incorporate all forms of grouping to support successful learning. Students need to be a part of many different groups. Sometimes the students might select their own group membership, while for other activities the teacher might assign group membership. In any case, group membership should be flexible and changing so as to allow the students to work with a diversity of peers and to avoid any students from being labeled based solely on their group membership. This flexible group membership also prevents some students from always being labeled the "helper" and others as always being labeled the "helped."

Classroom Climate

In addition to the physical arrangement and instructional grouping, the bonding or social interconnectedness of the teacher(s) and students in the class is equally important in providing a healthy classroom climate. Table 3.1 offers several suggestions for ways teachers might connect with their students in order to enhance the classroom climate as accepting and non-threatening.

First, one-to-one teacher time with every student should be built into the classroom day, as all students need individualized attention from the teacher in order to feel as if they are essential members of the classroom. The teacher must be involved with the students, not isolated from them. Teachers can accomplish this by using appropriate self-disclosure when it will ease or assist in the development of a better classroom climate. High expectations accompanied by a belief in the abilities of all students to learn are essential teacher behaviors in a classroom where the climate is conducive for student learning.

Likewise, recognizing differing abilities and modeling tolerance for such differences is a way of including students with developmental disabilities as well as valuing their unique abilities. Thus, an inclusive classroom focuses on the best for and from each student.

Finally, using rituals and traditions has been shown to assist in the development of a classroom climate that is inclusive and "comfortable" for all students. Remember that the teacher is the main facilitator in building a sense of community, safety, and tolerance in the classroom.

Tomlinson (1999) has proposed several characteristics of teaching and learning in healthy classroom environments (see Table 3.2). These components support the development of a classroom climate that is both conducive for learning and high achievement for all students, with or without exceptional needs.

Table 3.2 Components of a Healthy Classroom Environment

✐ The Teacher Appreciates Each Child as an Individual.
✐ The Teacher Remembers to Teach Whole Children.
✐ The Teacher Continues to Develop Expertise.
✐ The Teacher Links Students and Ideas.
✐ The Teacher Strives for Joyful Learning.
✐ The Teacher Offers High Expectations-and Lots of Ladders.
✐ The Teacher Helps Students Make Their Own Sense of Ideas.
✐ The Teacher Shares the Teaching with Students.
✐ The Teacher Clearly Strives for Student Independence.
✐ The Teacher Uses Positive Energy and Humor.
✐ "Discipline" Is More Covert than Overt.
Tomlinson, 1999, pp. 31-34.

How can the classroom climate be modified to support learning for students with developmental disabilities? A positive classroom environment allows students to experience a sense of personal accomplishment. It is "well known that students learn more when the school and the classroom environments are positive and supportive" (Mercer & Mercer, 2001, p. 39). According to Miller (2002), teachers must identify and implement multiple opportunities for students to succeed and then to recognize their successes.

Additionally, it is important that all students feel accepted and valued, from not only the teacher but also their peers. For students with developmental disabilities, it is imperative that teachers identify areas of concern within the classroom milieu and modify the classroom environment so that all students experience a supportive classroom environment.

Most professionals agree that social interactions support and assist in the enhancement of interactions between students, both with and without disabilities and their teachers. One method that can be used to create a more positive classroom environment is peer networks. Peer networks are "groups of individuals who demonstrate an interest in and an understanding of the individual with a disability and have impact on that person's life" (Bartlett et al., 2002, p. 305). An example of this method is the Circle of Friends (Forest & Lusthaus, 1989) that has been especially useful with students with developmental disabilities.

Summary

As Miller (2002) states "organizing the learning environment is a critical component of successful teaching and learning. Even the best content, taught with appropriate learning processes in mind, will be unsuccessful if the classroom environment is not conducive to learning" (p. 82). For students with developmental disabilities to have success in an inclusive classroom, teachers must be prepared to be flexible. Teachers must consider different ways of organizing the physical environment, of modifying instructional groups, and of establishing a positive learning environment for ALL students.

C H A P T E R

4

CONTENT MODIFICATIONS

Content modifications, or content transformations, are modifications that alter instructional curricula and/or materials to support student learning. General education teachers have long made a practice of modifying instructional materials for learners in the classroom who have such diverse characteristics as developmental disabilities, or backgrounds that place them as at-risk for school failure. In many cases modifications that teachers have used in the past are still appropriate for inclusive classrooms. However, the primary differences between past practices and contemporary inclusive education practices are the regularity and purposes surrounding these modifications.

For example, teachers have been accustomed to reducing the number of vocabulary words, reducing the complexity of the definitions, or providing word lists for a student with developmental disabilities. In the past these types of modifications have occurred on an "as needed basis" for students with disabilities but not as a regular component in planning instruction for any student who might need such modifications. In order for substantive student learning to be achieved, teachers in inclusive classes regularly review learner needs and then adjust the "degree" and "kind" of content modification to support the student. In this chapter, several examples of content modification, including curricular and instructional modifications, will be described. These include curricular decisions and such curricular modifications as text alteration, study guides, introduction of learning contracts, and development of activity stations.

Curricular Decisions and Modifications

What a teacher decides to teach is critical. Tomlinson (1999) suggested that what is taught and learned must have student relevance, enhance self-understanding, be authentic, have immediate usability, and enhance student empowerment in the present as well as the future. Tomlinson's suggestions are relevant for all students, and are especially important for students with developmental disabilities where an appropriate curriculum must be future focused, functional, and reflective of the general curriculum.

How can curricular decisions be modified to support learning for students with developmental disabilities? According to Janney and Snell (2000), curriculum and instruction are two of the areas that can be adapted so that students can "participate in a way that is personally meaningful" (p. 17). In fact, Webber (1997) suggested that, for students with mild/moderate disabilities, perhaps only the content of the curriculum may need adaptation. For those students with more severe disabilities, both the curriculum and the instructional strategies may need to be changed.

Curricular Changes

Janney and Snell (2000) described three types of modified curricula. These are: (a) supplementary curricula, (b) simplified curricula, and (c) alternative curricula.

Supplementary Curricula

One way to adapt the general curriculum for students with exceptional needs is to develop a supplementary curriculum. This may include the addition of basic skills or social and/or study skills, or the expansion of the curriculum for students with special learning or behavioral needs or students who are gifted and talented.

Simplified Curricula

Alternatively, curricula might be abridged for students with special needs. This modification results in students having the same objectives that are taught in a simpler way, or "by emphasizing fewer skills and concepts rather than the entire scope of the general curriculum" (Janney & Snell, 2000, p. 18).

Alternative Curricula

In some instances, the needs of the student require the development of an alternative curriculum, one that then partially or completely replaces the general curriculum. This alternative curriculum would be structured depending on the specific student needs.

Instructional Adaptations

Along with adaptation of the curriculum is adaptation of the instruction. This involves changes in "both the content and level of difficulty and the way that the information is provided" (Janney & Snell, 2000, p. 20).

The level of difficulty, or the amount of instruction, can be adapted in a variety of ways. These adaptations include the following:

- use of a variety of instructional methods, such as development of controlled vocabulary

- omission of extraneous details

- reduction of the readability level of text passages or test directions

- provision of additional cues, prompts, and feedback during practice activities

- inclusion of mini-lectures at 10 minute intervals

- development of chapter study guides for key concepts and vocabulary terms

- use of signals or choral responses for comprehension checking

- chunking of content into small segments

To adapt the manner in which instruction is given, the teacher has a number of possible options. For example, the teacher can:

- provide the student with outlines or lecture notes beforehand

- have the material read aloud

- accompany lectures with visual materials such as overheads, graphic organizers, and maps

- provide accompanying audio or videotapes

- highlight the essential ideas and facts in the text or handouts

- use hands-on activities

- include demonstrations of the assignments

- provide a central notebook of class calendar, homework assignments, class notes, study guides, and how-to-do lists (Janney & Snell, 2000; Kochhar, West, & Taymans, 2000).

According to Miller (2002), there are numerous research-validated accommodations that "enhance the delivery of instruction and therefore increase the likelihood that students with special learning needs will experience success in school" (pp. 292-293). These include:

- changing instructional cues

- using visual displays

- developing study guides

- utilizing instructional methods such as lecture-pause procedures, concept teaching routines, peer tutoring, cooperative learning, and computer-based instruction.

Multilevel Instruction

One planning strategy that is useful for teachers to more effectively accommodate all students within an inclusive classroom is that of multilevel instruction. Multilevel instruction is defined as "an approach to teaching that engages all students in the class in the same curricular areas, but with differing goals and varying levels of difficulty" (Miller, 2002, p. 300). According to Bartlett et al. (2002), "this strategy has been effective with students with mental disabilities because it focuses on developing concepts by using content as a means for teaching specific skills, rather than teaching the content as an end in itself" (p. 304).

This type of instruction uses numerous methods of teacher presentation and also various types of practice so that the differing ability levels within an inclusive classroom can all be accommodated. As such, it holds great promise for improving the quality of instruction for all students (Bartlett et al., 2002).

According to Miller (2002) two strategies effective for students with developmental disabilities are (a) curriculum overlapping, and (b) tiered assignments. Curriculum overlapping allows students to share an activity while addressing different learning outcomes. This method is useful in imbedding functional curriculum skills into the general curriculum. Tiered assignments can be used when teachers are able to identify the requisite concepts and develop diverse assignments that differ in difficulty level depending on the needs of the students in the specific class.

Text Alteration

For students with developmental disabilities, typical classroom texts and other written materials often have a readability level that is too difficult for them to successfully navigate. Even when students may otherwise be able to understand the content, the reading level of the written material may be a barrier to learning, especially in content area textbooks.

According to Salend (2001), there are a number of methods by which the readability of the material may be adjusted to meet the needs of the students. These methods include modifying the content of the material, simplifying the text, and using electronic forms of the material. Salend (2001) also suggests highlighting information in the textbook so that critical information is noted. Picture codes can be used to help identify and rate important materials for the student (e.g., placing symbols in the margin of the text). Key words can be circled or otherwise identified.

Simplifying materials can be time consuming for teachers but has been shown to assist those students with learning difficulties who are included in the general education classroom. One especially useful method of simplifying the text offered by Hoover and Patton (1997) is to cover the page with transparency material and mark out the difficult words with a marker, placing the simplified text above. This allows the student to use the same textbook, read at a more appropriate level, but also have a visual comparison of the higher readability text.

If the student with developmental disabilities is unable to access even simplified written materials, then electronic forms of the text may be required. According to Schumm (1999), audio taping books and other classroom materials can provide students with access to information so that they can continue to learn vocabulary and concepts. Audio taped books are available from commercial bookstores, from non-profit organizations such as public libraries, or can be prepared by the teacher or other support personnel. It should be remembered that the use of audio taping of materials is not a substitute for learning to read, but a support activity to assist the student in continuing to learn the curricular content.

Study Guides

The use of a study guide can lead students through a reading assignment. A study guide is a set of questions, fragments, or words that students complete or define while reading assigned materials. The study guide points to the important facts of the text while providing an organizational structure that directs the student to the important facts. Bos and Vaughn (2002) suggested the following guidelines:

1. Decide whether a guide is needed.

2. Analyze the chapter.

3. Decide how you want to structure your study guide.

Suggested components of a study guide include:

- Specific information about the reading assignments (page numbers, title)
- Learning objectives of the assignments
- Purpose statement for the assignment
- Introduction of key terms or vocabulary
- Activities for students to complete
- Questions for students to answer as they read

(Bos & Vaughn, 2002, p. 302)

Learning Contracts

In order to promote a sense of independence for all students, a teacher might use a learning contract. A learning contract is a written agreement made between the student and the teacher that includes the specified task, the requirements for successful completion and any rules for conduct students must follow when working on their contracts. A learning contract can provide an opportunity to include student choice in the selection of sequence and tasks that the learner is to complete. Its specificity and concrete nature may make learning contracts especially useful for students with developmental disabilities.

An in-depth knowledge of each student's readiness level, learning profile and interests assists the teacher in designing the content of the learning tasks that will promote student growth. Tomlinson (1999) outlines several components teachers should consider in designing learning contracts (see Table 4.1).

Table 4.1   Considerations in Designing Learning Contracts

> ✎ Assumes it is the teacher's responsibility to specify important learnings and make sure students acquire them.
>
> ✎ Assumes students can take on some of the responsibility for learning themselves.
>
> ✎ Delineates skills that need to be practiced and mastered.
>
> ✎ Ensures students will apply or use those skills in context.
>
> ✎ Specifies working conditions to which students must adhere during the contract time (student behavior, time constraints, homework and classwork involvement in the contract).
>
> ✎ Sets positive consequences (continued freedom, grades) when students adhere to working conditions. It also sets negative consequences (teacher makes work assignments and sets working parameters) if students do not adhere to working conditions.
>
> ✎ Establishes criteria for successful completion and quality of work.
>
> ✎ Includes signatures of agreement.
>
> Tomlinson, 1999, p.87.

Activity Stations

Another modification that may be helpful for teachers in meeting the needs of students with developmental disabilities is the use of activity stations in the classroom. Activity stations involve setting up different locations throughout the classroom where students may work on a selected learning activity that supports the lesson of the day.

According to Remus and Adcock (1998), activity stations, also known as in-class learning stations, can be used when whole class activities are such that even with adaptation the students would not be able to participate in a meaningful way. Thus the activity station becomes an example of a parallel activity for enhancing the learning of a student who has developmental disabilities.

Since the students are not required to complete all classroom activity stations, this is a method of addressing different learner needs through the task selection, flexible grouping, and student movement. All students may work at a particular station that has been designed to address different learning objectives selected for the individual learner at some point during the day, period or week.

Summary

Content modifications assist teachers in addressing individual learner needs while moving all students forward in learning the important content. Modification of the content also helps the teacher take the curricular standards required for a grade level or subject and transforms them to "fit" the learner. This transformation can assist in reducing anxiety or boredom in the lives of children with exceptional needs. As Miller (2002) notes:

> The number of students needing modifications to gain access to and benefit from the general curriculum has increased as American classrooms have become more inclusive and more diverse. Thus, teachers are challenged to find effective and efficient ways to meet the varying needs of all their students...(p. 326)

This is particularly true as students with developmental disabilities are included into the general education classroom, and provided greater and more effective access to the general education curriculum.

CHAPTER

5

PROCESS MODIFICATIONS

One might argue that making process modifications is an instructional strategy. This chapter thus might be considered a "Part 2" in presenting options teachers might use in an inclusive classroom. Like those modifications described in the previous chapters, the process modifications described in this chapter should not be viewed as a prescription or a recipe to follow. Rather, it is a means of identifying a better "fit" between diverse students and the curriculum and learning environment.

What Instructional Strategies Are Effective?

Teachers often would like a basic and general guide to assist them in initially thinking about strategies appropriate for use in their inclusive classrooms. Tomlinson (1995) provided such a guide to assist teachers in designing strategies that are more likely to assure the success of all students in inclusive settings, including students with developmental disabilities (see Table 5.1).

Table 5.1   Guide to Designing Strategy Modifications

> ✐ Have a clear purpose.
>
> ✐ Focus on a few key ideas.
>
> ✐ Guide them in understanding the ideas and the relationships among them.
>
> ✐ Offer opportunities to explore ideas through varied modes (e.g., visual, kinesthetic, spatial, musical).
>
> ✐ Help them relate new information to previous understanding.
>
> ✐ Match their level of readiness.
>
> Tomlinson, 1995, p. 53.

In addition, Remus and Adcock (1998) provided additional options that teachers can employ to promote successful inclusion of students with disabilities (see Table 5.2).

Table 5.2   Adapting Curricula & Instruction in Inclusive Settings

Setting up lessons
- Lecture, demonstration, and practice
- Whole-class discussion
- Small groups and peer partnerships
- Games, simulations, role playing, presentations, and activity based lessons
- Community instruction

Adapting instruction
- Change the learning goals
- Change the learning environment
- Change the materials
- Change the way students express what they know
- Allow students more time to perform
- Change how much or what kind of personal assistance students get
- Create an alternative activity

Remus & Adcock, 1998.

Still other possibilities include:

- Tiered lessons

- Entry points

- Learning centers

- Cubing

- Choice boards

- Tic-Tac-Toe menu

- RAFT strategy

- Independent projects

- Instructional technology

These are described below.

Tiered Lessons

Tiered lessons refers to an instructional strategy where the focus of the activities is the same for all students, but the activities are adjusted by using different levels of complexity, abstraction, and open-endedness. Tiered lessons are used by teachers who have a clear focus of what is essential for students to know, understand and be able to do in a particular subject. This type of lesson design ensures that all students gain the needed understandings while being challenged according to their abilities (Tomlinson, 1999).

To design a tiered lesson, the teacher begins with deciding the specific content that students should know, understand and be able to do. The teacher then considers the range of learners present in the class. The teacher then determines what might be an appropriate learning task that would be rich, challenging and engaging and would help the students come to understand the content. The teacher evaluates the learning task to determine for whom the lesson is a "fit."

Next, the teacher determines how many additional versions of the lesson are needed to meet the various learning needs in the classroom. This might be one, two, three or more versions that better allow specific learners to successfully connect with the concepts being addressed. The advantage of developing tiered lessons is that all students have an opportunity to explore essential ideas and concepts, but in a way that recognizes that different learners can handle various levels of complexity, structure and open-endedness.

Entry Points

Gardner (1991, 1993) developed a strategy, known as entry points, to address different intelligence preferences when learners are exploring topics of interest. This strategy capitalizes on the strengths inherent in each learner's specific learning preference. Tomlinson (1999) described five avenues or entry points that teachers might utilize:

- Narrational Entry Point: Presenting a story or narrative about the topic or concept in question.

- Logical-Quantitative Entry Point: Using numbers or deductive/ scientific approaches to the topic or question.

- Foundational Entry Point: Examining the philosophy and vocabulary that undergird the topic or concept.

- Aesthetic Entry Point: Focusing on the sensory features of the topic or concept.

- Experiential Entry Point: Using a hands-on approach where the student deals directly with materials that represent the topic or concept. These materials also make links to the student's personal experience.

Learning Centers

A learning center is a classroom area that contains a collection of activities or materials designed to teach, reinforce, or extend a particular skill or concept (Kaplan, Kaplan, Madsen & Gould, 1980). The important idea for teachers who are using learning centers in an inclusive classroom is that there must be a variety of learning tasks within each center. In addition, there must be a system of connecting learner needs and interests with specific centers. In other words, if the expectation is that all students would do all activities in all centers, it is unlikely that the learning center effectively addresses different learner needs.

Cubing

Cubing is another instructional strategy that can assist the teacher with checking for understanding while increasing interest and motivation for all students. The idea behind a cubing exercise is a review of a unit or topic that the students have recently studied in the class.

The teacher first identifies several tasks he or she believes would be appropriate for the topic. Then, starting from a list of commands such as "describe," "compare," "associate," "analyze," "apply," "argue," "rearrange," "illustrate," "question," "evaluate," "connect," "cartoon," "change," "solve," "list," "chart," "make," etc., the teacher chooses six of these.

The teacher next decides appropriate prompts, or supplementary cues, to include under each of the six commands. The specific learners in the classroom should be taken into account when designing the various prompts that further explains the command to students.

Each of these commands is then placed on one of six sides of a cube, or large die. The cubes may be designed and color-coded for different groups of students with all students working on the same commands but having different prompts.

For example, every cube may have a "describe" command. However, the prompt for that command for one group might ask them to use pictures and words describing a character or an event. The prompt for that command for another group might ask them to develop a concept map. The prompt for that command for still another group might ask them to write a story or essay. Then the teacher should decide the rules for the students (for example, "Do all six sides," "Roll and do any four sides," "Do the required two sides and choose two others," etc.) Another recommendation for designing cubes is have at least one easy task and one hard task identified for each cube regardless of the student's readiness level. This will help build confidence and competence.

Choice Boards

Another modification that a teacher might utilize in order to modify the curriculum for students with developmental disabilities is choice boards. The use of student choice in selection of activities, or the method of implementation or completion of the selected activity, provides a student with control over his/her learning. This not only allows for student self-direction but also has been noted as one way to reduce student/teacher power struggles (Hoover & Patton, 1997).

A choice board can be a bulletin board or a display board that uses pockets that are labeled or color-coded. A variety of tasks cards are placed in each pocket (Tomlinson, 1999). The task cards delineate an assignment a student should complete. The element of choice is implemented through teacher design. The options might include pockets wherein a student has a choice of completing one or more of the tasks cards found in that pocket, or the teacher may offer choices of pockets from which a student may choose a specific activity. In a differentiated classroom, an experienced teacher would carefully strive for a balance of some student-selected and teacher-selected activities through the use of the choice board.

Tic-Tac-Toe Menu

A Tic-Tac-Toe menu is a form of choice board combined with a learning contract. In this strategy the teacher designs a number of learning tasks that are placed on the Tic-Tac-Toe menu. From this menu the students choose the direction (horizontally, vertically, or diagonally) they would like to travel to form a Tic-Tac-Toe. The students are also given the option of completing an alternate choice with the teacher's permission or do additional activities for extra credit.

RAFT Strategy

The RAFT strategy is a writing activity that employs higher order thinking skills and nontraditional written products. RAFT is an acronym that stands for:

- Role of the writer. What is the writer's role: reporter, observer, eyewitness?

- Audience. Who will be reading this writing: the teacher, other students, a parent, people in the community, an editor?

- Format. What is the best way to present this writing: in a letter, an article, a report, a poem?

- Topic. Who or what is the subject of this writing: a famous mathematician, a prehistoric cave dweller, a reaction to a specific event?

Billmeyer and Barton (1998) explain the RAFT strategy in this way: "Instead of writing a traditional essay explaining a concept learned, students demonstrate their understanding in a nontraditional format. This technique encourages creative thinking and motivates students to reflect in unusual ways about concepts they have read" (p. 151).

Independent Projects

A strategy that supports student learning and also recognizes the needs of diverse learners is independent projects. While independent projects have long been recommended as an appropriate strategy for advanced learners (Shore, Cornell, Robinson, & Ward, 1991), it can be an appropriate strategy for all learners. All learners need to apply concepts, information and skills that they have learned while also exploring topics in which they may have an interest. Utilizing the independent project strategy is one means of capitalizing on student interest and providing another vehicle for students to demonstrate what they have come to learn. Tomlinson and Imbeau (1999) have generated an extensive list of questions concerning various facets of the process that may assist teachers in guiding their students with their independent projects. These are outlined below.

I. Selecting a Topic

A. What are the content parameters for the project? Have you stated clearly what the student should come to know, understand, and be able to do as a result of the independent study?

B. Once the student has selected a preliminary topic, did you have him/her "graze" among resources to see whether enough information (or too much) exists on the topic, whether the topic will have staying power for the student, and whether the student can understand the topic in a reasonable way?

C. Have you guided the student to do a cursory survey to understand important sub-topics or issues, essential information about them, and key questions that must be asked in order to probe the topic appropriately?

D. Have you helped the student focus and pose an actual question(s) to investigate?

II. Use of Resources

A. Are the range and types of resources the student uses important? If so, make that clear.

B. Have you helped the student think about resource quality?

C. Have you helped the student know how to keep track of sources and the data from those sources?

D. Have you helped the student know how to synthesize information and ideas (vs. stringing facts together without personal understanding)?

III. Planning the Quest

A. Should the student use a mentor? What will the mentor's role be? Should there be a written agreement with the mentor?

B. Do you need to see the data? In what format? Do you want to see the student's final research question(s)?

C. Should you and the student draw up a timeline for all phases of the independent study?

D. Should the student keep a process log or diary of what he/she is thinking and how she is working?

E. Will you suggest a range of possible modes of presenting findings (e.g., a drama, video, photo essay or formal speech)? Students would benefit from an explanation of each option.

F. Will there be a formal presentation to a school audience or a "real" audience beyond the classroom? How and when will it be set up?

IV. Supporting Documents

A. Will you provide the student with a set of instructions or other "readmit" for the project?

B. Should you develop guidelines for student behavior while working independently (e.g., when the student must be in class vs. working in another location)?

C. Will you send an informational letter to parents explaining the nature of the project, guidelines for positive parent support, timelines, etc.? Can the student play a role in developing explanations for parents?

V. Criteria for Success

A. What criteria for success will you develop related to content, thinking, planning, persistence, presentation? How will the criteria help the student understand growth toward excellence and expertise? Will the mentor play a role in establishing professional level criteria?

B. What criteria for success will the student develop? Does he or she need any samples or models of criteria?

C. Will this investigation be related to letter grades? Has that been clearly explained?

Instructional Technology

The recent and ongoing rapid expansion of technology in the schools has resulted in an equivalent growth in instructional options for teachers. These options include computers and computer-assisted instruction, hypertext/hypermedia teaching systems, videocassette recorders and videodiscs, digital cameras, CD-ROM based materials, and captioned television programs. In addition some students with developmental disabilities may benefit from such assistive devices as high technology computer communication systems, or low technology systems such as communication boards.

Many school districts have computer labs where (particularly at the elementary level) each class is scheduled to attend on a regular basis. It is effective to have students working on a self-directed activities in such areas as reading, writing and mathematics, if the teacher first becomes familiar with the programs the school has available. The pace of instruction can be adjusted to best fit individual student characteristics and needs.

In addition, technology can help teachers as they assess student skill levels. This facilitates data-driven instructional choices and decisions.

Summary

This chapter provided a guide for identifying educational strategies that facilitate successful inclusion. In addition, it outlined nine specific instructional procedures that teachers have found to be effective in enhancing the success of all students, including those with developmental disabilities, in inclusive settings.

Needless to say, there are countless other strategies that are appropriate for inclusive classrooms. The purpose of presenting some of these instructional strategies has been to demonstrate how a variety of techniques, some of which were originally developed for gifted education programs, can easily be adapted to be used with all students, including those with developmental disabilities, in inclusive education classrooms. The ability of a teacher to see a variety of educational possibilities in any given instructional technique is a hallmark of successful education.

C H A P T E R

6

PRODUCT MODIFICATIONS

Student progress reporting and monitoring is an essential facet of teacher responsibility for all students (Miller, 2002), and perhaps especially for students with disabilities. For these students, each IEP includes progress information on benchmarks or short-term objectives leading to successful completion of the IEP annual goals.

In order for the teacher to assess whether student learning has occurred, some form of product, or observable outcome of that learning, must occur. According to Tomlinson (1999), "products are vehicles through which students demonstrate and extend what they have learned" (p. 11). In other words, the product is the culmination of the learning activity, lesson, unit, or an outcome of the learning experiences that the teacher presents (Renzulli, Leppien, & Hays, 2000).

The issue for teachers is that the typical product format or assessment system used in general education classrooms may not be effective in accurately assessing the knowledge level of students with diverse learning needs, including developmental disabilities. Just as some students may require modifications in the learning environment, content, and process, they and others may also need different ways to demonstrate their success in learning the content.

Types of Planned Outcomes

When designing a lesson with its subsequent assessment component, two types of outcomes can be considered (Renzulli, Leppien, & Hayes, 2000). These are concrete products and abstract products.

Concrete Products

Concrete products are physical constructions created by students for the evaluation of student learning. These include such instructional outcomes as essays, videos, dramatizations, and experiments. Renzulli et al. (2000) grouped concrete products into seven categories. These include:

- artistic products
- performance products
- spoken products
- visual products
- models/construction products
- leadership products
- written products

Each of these is described below.

Artistic products

Artistic products are those in which student learning is exhibited through creative and graphic development of a physical product. Examples of artistic products include murals, filmstrips, drawings, photographs, mobiles, diorama, collage, paints, pottery, and maps.

Performance products

The second category is performance products that evaluate student knowledge through student development and performance. Performance products include skits, role-playing, mime, puppet shows, musical performance, reenactments, and interpretive song.

Spoken products

Spoken products are those products where the student presents learned information in an oral format. This category of products includes speeches, poetry readings, songs, announcements, newscasts, oral reports, sign language, and rap songs.

Visual products

Visual products are the fourth category, and in some ways overlap with the previous three categories. Visual products include videos, book jackets, models, computer programs, diagrams, set design, and photography.

Model/construction products

Products that incorporate building or construction of a model for evaluation make up the category known as model/construction products. Examples of this category are relief maps, terrariums, diorama, ant farms, birdhouses, bulletin boards, 3-D figures, robots, machines, and furniture.

Leadership products

Another category is leadership products. Activities in this category are designed to help students learn and demonstrate leadership skills. These activities include giving a speech, role playing, participating in a debate, organizing a business or a fundraising event, editing a newspaper, and hosting a chat room or discussion group on the Internet.

Written products

The final category is written products. In this category students exhibit their knowledge in the form of a written product. Examples include brochures, captions, charts, interview questions, recipes, newspaper articles, web pages, lists, timelines, story problems, and graphic organizers.

Abstract Products

Sometimes evaluation through a concrete product presentation is not feasible. In these cases evaluation of knowledge may need to occur through abstract products.

Abstract products are specific student behaviors identified by the teacher as indicators to verify that student learning has occurred. Abstract products are generally divided into two categories: cognitive structures and affective structures.

Abstract products in the cognitive structures are identified through teacher observation of such student behaviors as the use of meta-cognition, perseverance in completing a project and problem-solving strategies. The affective category is also evaluated through teacher observation and includes observations of the student's empathy for others, self-concept, and appreciation. This category might also include data on the behavioral and social skills that are more and more critical in many student IEPs. (For a more expanded list of both concrete and abstract products, see Renzulli et al., 2000, "Instructional Products Menu", pp. 68-69.)

Options in Assessment

In order to most effectively meet the needs of students with exceptional needs in the inclusive classroom, assessment procedures that are more comprehensive and powerful than are traditional paper and pencil tests in evaluating student learning should be used. Mercer and Mercer (2001) noted that common assessment options include commercial tests, curriculum tests, portfolios, criterion-referenced skill inventories and checklists, and teacher-made instruction (p. 101). These options tend to be more norm-referenced, and thus may not be particularly instructionally useful for students with developmental disabilities.

Alternatives to these assessment procedures include authentic assessment, portfolio assessment, and presentations such as work samples, class projects, and videotapes of student performance, and scoring guides or rubrics. These alternatives hold considerable promise for generating richer and more educationally useful information for teachers, and are further described below.

Authentic Assessment

Authentic assessment is a form of alternative assessment that includes measures based in the real world in order to allow students to demonstrate their knowledge and skills (Webber, 1997). In authentic assessment, meaningful, complex, and relevant learning activities are included in the assessment process, with student performance assessed through different avenues and formats. Authentic assessments include demonstrations, projects, and presentations (Salend, 2001). Although some individuals believe that authentic assessment can only be completed outside the school, others disagree. As the school is the "real-world" for students, many consider authentic assessment appropriate for any classroom or other school environment.

Portfolio Assessment

Portfolios can be an especially useful form of authentic assessment. According to Batzle (1992), portfolios are a "visual presentation of a student's capabilities, strengths, weaknesses, accomplishments and progress" (p. 12). Since portfolios are easily tailored to meet specific student needs, they can be considered extremely versatile (Mastropieri & Scruggs, 2000).

According to Webber (1997), portfolios can be used both for instruction and for assessment. Portfolios are constructed as teachers and students work together collecting and reflecting on student products over a specified period of time. The type and number of products to be included in the portfolio should also be decided on in an interactive dialogue between the student and the teacher.

Examples of portfolio products include book logs, student self-evaluations, math projects, results from examinations, video tapes or photographs of science experiments, individually developed semantic maps or graphic organizers, research reports. (For a more extensive list of potential products for inclusion in portfolios, see Miller, 2002, p. 362-363).

Miller (2002) lists five steps in this form of assessment. These are as follows.

1. identification of the purpose of the portfolio

2. selection of the specific type of portfolio

3. development of the portfolio assessment plan

4. collection and organization of the student products

5. evaluation of the student performance (p. 357)

In addition, teachers who are considering using portfolios in instruction and evaluation of students might incorporate the six basic principles of portfolio assessment and evaluation identified in Table 6.1. (See Bos & Vaughn, 2002, p. 307 for additional suggestions for developing portfolios to monitor student progress, and examples of items that can be included in portfolios.)

Table 6.1   Basic Principles of Portfolio Assessment and Evaluation

> ✐ Portfolio assessment and evaluation is ongoing and gathered over time.
>
> ✐ Portfolio assessment and evaluation embraces different developmental levels.
>
> ✐ Portfolio assessment and evaluation matches and guides instruction.
>
> ✐ Portfolio assessment and evaluation is unique to each child.
>
> ✐ (Table continued from previous page.) Portfolio assessment and evaluation emphasizes what kids know.
>
> ✐ Portfolio assessment and evaluation involves teachers and children conferencing and evaluating together.
>
> ✐ Portfolio assessment and evaluation provides a variety of evidence through process and product samples.
>
> Batzle, 1992, pp. 13-19.

Scoring Guides or Rubrics

Scoring guides or rubrics are typically discussed alongside authentic and performance assessment, and portfolio assessment. According to Batzle (1992), a rubric is a form of scoring guide that is designed to assess student work within a specific curricular area. More specifically, rubrics are defined as "statements specifying the criteria associated with different levels of proficiency for evaluating student performance" (Salend, 2001, p. 426). The major reason for using a scoring guide or rubric when evaluating students is that the grading of modified products can be made more objective and consistent.

Rubrics can be either individually or interactively developed. Individually developed rubric are usually prepared by the teacher, while an interactively developed rubric is jointly developed by teacher and student. Developing a rubric is a two-step process.

The first step is to decide on the facets or components of the rubric; that is, what knowledge should be evaluated. The second component, a decision on the rating scale size and criteria, is more difficult, as "no set rules exist for evaluating the contents of a portfolio" (Miller, 2002, p. 359).

Generally the grading scales on rubrics are structured with three levels: (a) below expectations, (b) meets expectations, and (c) exceeds expectations. For each level, a clear, concise set of criteria is developed.

Students with developmental disabilities may need assistance in understanding the criteria and their use. Concrete examples are especially helpful as guides.

Summary

Many teachers who incorporate differentiated instructional methods into their classes are concerned with the evaluation of those students with exceptional needs. The issue of "fair" evaluation practices that do not lessen the quality of the curriculum for all students continues to be of concern. This is especially true for those students with developmental disabilities who are included into general education classrooms.

Both concrete products and abstract products can provide valuable evaluative information. Authentic assessment, especially portfolio assessment, can be especially useful in determining educational progress and success in students with developmental disabilities. The incorporation of scoring rubrics in these can further enhance the validity and reliability of the evaluation procedures.

CHAPTER

7

PUTTING IT ALL TOGETHER

Teachers in inclusive classrooms need practical and effective strategies for meeting the diverse learning needs of their diverse students, including those with developmental disabilities. This book has provided an overview of differentiated instruction to assist teachers in examining their personal beliefs concerning teaching and learning, and has offered practical suggestions that might be appropriate for use in inclusive classrooms.

To help "put it all together," here are examples of three teachers who want to develop differentiated instruction practices in inclusive classrooms. Perhaps their journeys will offer answers to typical questions that arise when considering whether to use differentiated instruction.

Educator 1: Sally

Sally is an elementary school classroom teacher who has been teaching for four years. She is presently working on her master's degree in Curriculum and Instruction with an emphasis in the education of gifted and talented children. She has a classroom of 25 first graders in a school located in a "bedroom" community near a large midwestern city. The school district has recently adopted a philosophy of inclusion, with the general education classroom the primary placement for all students with exceptional needs.

At the present time Sally's class includes 11 boys and 14 girls, ranging in age from 6 to 9 years old. Of these 25 students, there are 3 for whom English is not the primary language, 2 who have been officially identified as gifted and talented, 4 who receive special education services, and 1 who is on a Section 504 accommodation plan.

Of the 4 students who are on IEPs, 3 students (Mark, Cindy and Brian) are diagnosed with learning disabilities, and 1 student (Diana) has moderate mental retardation and cerebral palsy. The 1 student (John) on a Section 504 accommodation plan has been diagnosed with attention deficit hyperactivity disorder.

Learning Environment Considerations

As Sally reviews the Planning Pyramid and the areas to be considered when differentiating instruction for a mixed-ability classroom, she decides to focus first on her classroom environment. The issues that must be addressed are physical accessibility (both within the classroom and the school), the social structure of the classroom (including grouping arrangements), and the development of leadership for all students. What should Sally concentrate on first? She decides to first examine the current physical arrangement of her room.

The students' desks in Sally's classroom are in rows except for two tables on the side of the class near her own desk. These two tables are the "desks" for Diana and John. For most of the day, Diana and John sit at one or both of these tables where they receive help from a teacher assistant. Diana leaves the classroom for occupational therapy and a speech therapist comes in periodically to help Diana with her picture communication board. For the most part John sits at the table away from the other students because he is easily distracted and needs redirection by his teacher assistant. Occasionally he displays some oppositional behaviors.

For most of Sally's lessons, she uses "whole group" instruction followed by independent seatwork and sometimes paired-group work. Sally quickly realizes that her class arrangement facilitates independence but not social or leadership interactions. In fact, she notes that two of her students, Diana and John, are not even part of her "whole group" and therefore, have limited, if any, peer interactions during the school day.

Group Seating Arrangement

The first thing Sally decides is that she would like to have the students' desks arranged in groups of five. Also, since her class has diverse abilities, she will plan mixed-ability grouping for her seating arrangement. Having done a learning profile for each student she knows her students well. Sally is confident that she can appropriately select students for each group. She plans to group students using different student characteristics such as common interests, varying social and leadership skills, and varying abilities and background knowledge and experiences.

Sally also decides that she will try to keep this seating arrangement for at least three months. She would like each group of students to get to know each other well, and to have a stable "home" group to return to when she first tries other types of grouping arrangements for classroom instruction.

She also knows that she will place Diana next to and across from her peers, and will place John on the end-side of the five desk grouping so that his desk will not be as closely aligned with the others. She will try a desk divider to use when he is too distracted by the activity and/or other students. If he needs to move his desk slightly away, or turn it completely around, from the group he will be easily able to do so. Also, his "old" desk, the table by the sidewall, will be right behind him so that he can turn his chair around and use the table when needed.

Up until this time, Sally has grouped her students only for reading instruction. She has a reading corner, so she has placed students together for reading based on their reading levels. Sally believes she needs to more closely monitor her reading readiness groups to ensure student movement among the groups.

She further believes that grouping her students sometimes by interests instead of by levels of academic achievement can enhance student learning. Sally also believes she should focus on her students' needs in mathematics to see if various types of flexible grouping arrangements might be appropriate.

Flexible Grouping Using Cooperative Learning

After reviewing her physical arrangements, Sally realizes that her focus on differentiated instruction in mathematics begins with her need to use flexible grouping arrangements. She would like to start using cooperative learning because of her interest in developing social and leadership skills within her class. Sally decides to start with cooperative learning group skills, including learning how (a) to give positive feedback to each other, (b) to take turns, and (c) to listen to and encourage/cue for peer responses. She will start slowly in mathematics with one social skill at a time. She plans to develop activities to help emphasize the particular social or leadership development skill she is working on for that particular time period.

Since Sally has had little experience with cooperative learning, she will start small, beginning with groups of three. Sally will form eight mathematics groups consisting of three students each, except for one group which will have four students. When she and her students become comfortable with working in groups of three, she then will introduce larger group arrangements.

Content Modifications

Sally asks herself, "How should the content be modified in order to address the needs of all students?" In mathematics, Sally has been working on one of the school district standards for first grade, "Understanding the concept of time." To this point her lessons have addressed goals and objectives related to (a) telling time to the hour, minute, and second, and (b) solving time-related problems. Even though the majority of her students have been part of these whole group lessons, many of them have not been successful.

Sally decides to review the content related to the concept of telling time and determine how she will include all students in her mathematics lessons on time. She plans to change her instructional method from whole-class instruction and individual seatwork activities to differentiated instructional activities based on individual student readiness levels.

Sally will assess her students with a curriculum-based criterion referenced inventory to determine what time-telling skills each student has mastered and which skills each student needs to develop. Since Diana, her student with moderate mental retardation, requires additional background experiences and skills to learn how to tell time, Sally will implement an alternative curriculum for Diana, using curriculum overlapping.

Diana has a number of objectives from her IEP that can be incorporated in the telling time mathematics lessons. For example, she is learning to match numbers from one to five, to take turns, to use turning motions such as turning doorknobs and keys in doors, and to initiate requests using her picture communication board.

Another student, Brian, who has been identified as having a specific learning disability in mathematics, is learning to count by fives and recognizing numbers from 1-50. His content will be simplified to accommodate his number skills and readiness to tell time. Sally expects that after all students are assessed, a few other students may need the content modified.

Process Modifications

After assessing her students, Sally decides to use learning centers and multilevel instruction. Her mathematics-learning center on telling time will include a variety of materials and tasks at different levels of readiness. Activities will be color-coded and numbered to reflect the knowledge and experience required for completing each activity.

Also, Sally will set up learning center contracts with each student. In structuring these contracts she will choose some activities that each student will complete, and will allow students to choose some activities for themselves. A time line will be developed for each student to keep track of his/her own activities and schedules for completion.

Sally will also plan a number of multilevel instructional activities to be incorporated in her group activities. For example, Diana will be placed with two other students. Each student within the group will have his or her own color cards. These cards will be shuffled. As each student's color card comes up on the pile, that student will perform the task requested on the card. One student will be the checker, one student will be the facilitator, and the third student will be the encourager.

Diana's cards will be read by another student in her group. Some of her tasks are based on her IEP objectives. For example, Diana will be requested to turn the hands of the clock. When she stops, another student in the group must tell the time to the hour, minute and/or second. Diana will also be requested to point to the correct number (1, 2 or 3) on her desk when another student in her group points to the associated number on the clock. Also, before receiving the clock for her turn, Diana will initiate or be requested to point to the clock on her picture communication board.

Brian will also need similar accommodations to his tasks cards and activities during these group lessons and practice sessions. His tasks will reflect his entry point in the instruction. Some students within the group will have entry points that require higher level thinking skills. Their tasks in the groups will be more advanced, as they will be expected to perform such tasks as indicating what time it will be in 3 minutes, 35 minutes; giving the correct time using pictures of analog clocks without numbers; and solving word problems using such time terminology as "quarter past the hour."

Product Modifications

Sally plans to use three types of evaluation to check students' understanding of the concept of time. First, she will develop checklists for the checker in each group to record data. Each student's checklist will reflect the tasks that the individual performs in the group and at the learning center. Sally will move from group to group to give individual and group instruction, and also to listen to the students' verbal responses and monitor their performance as indicated on their checklists.

Second, Sally will request that each student select one activity related to time that he or she has completed at the learning center. This time concept activity should be one the student can demonstrate to the class indicating successful learning of the concept. The products will vary from student to student, and may include such products as drawings, demonstrations, oral reports, practice worksheets with answer keys, and "time" games.

Third, Sally will use authentic assessment. She will check each student on time-related problems in real life situations at school throughout the unit on time to assess generalization and application of the time concepts that each student is learning. She will use varying levels of questions to elicit responses. Diana will be allowed to use her picture communication board to provide her answer.

Educator 2: Frank

Frank is a middle level classroom teacher in the areas of Mathematics and Science. Although he has taught for five years in this district situated in a rural community, this is his first year teaching at a middle school. This year the administrators in the school district decided to expand the inclusion philosophy from the elementary level to the middle school level. As a result, the middle school teachers have been grouped into pods, with each pod containing one Mathematics/Science teacher, one English/Social Studies teacher, one related arts teacher (P.E., Art, or Music) and one Special Education teacher. Cooperative teaching (e.g., Hourcade & Bauwens, 2002) by team members is emphasized.

There are 75 middle level students in grades 6 through 8. Frank's pod is responsible for 24 students matriculating through the seventh grade. At the present time Frank's class includes 14 boys and 10 girls, ranging in age from 11 to 14 years old. Of these 24 students, there are 2 for whom

English is not the primary language, 3 who have been identified as gifted and talented, and 5 who receive special education services. Of those 5 students receiving special education services, 2 students have been identified as having mental retardation (Danny has severe mental retardation and Janis has mild mental retardation); 2 students, Maria and Jamie, have been identified as having learning disabilities; and 1 student, Mark, has been identified as having an emotional/behavioral disability.

As Frank reviews the Planning Pyramid and the areas to be considered when using differentiated instruction in a mixed-ability classroom, he decides to focus first on the process involved; that is, the instructional strategies that will need to be modified. The issues that must be addressed are the safety issues involved in teaching science, the methodological and philosophical differences involved in teaching through an experiential/ constructivist approach, the use of manipulatives to enhance learning for adolescents, and the issues of concrete versus critical thinking as the focus of instruction.

Although this is the first time that Frank has had a student with severe disabilities in his class, he has had students with various mild disabilities in his science classes in the past. He has made a number of modifications to the curriculum over the years but he often feels overwhelmed in trying to teach the academic content to all students. This year his goals are (a) to focus on reasonable objectives for each student and (b) to include Danny, his student with severe disabilities, in as many science activities as possible.

Frank decides that before he plans his lessons for his next unit in life science, he needs to respond to the three questions of the planning pyramid:

1. What will ALL students learn?

2. What will MOST but not all students learn?

3. What will SOME students learn?

The theme of the next unit is introducing cells. Frank decides that at the end of this unit ALL students will know the three parts of the cell theory, and will know and be able to label the two types of cells (prokaryotic and eukaryotic cells). MOST students will be able to describe the function of each component of these types of cells. They will be able to compare and contrast animal and plant cells. SOME students will be able to distinguish between an organism and a community of cells.

Learning Environment Considerations

Frank must address the environment in the classroom and how it needs to be modified in order to assure successful learning for all students. He determines that the highest environmental consideration is his student grouping arrangements.

Flexible grouping

Since this is the beginning unit on cells, many students in Frank's class have not used a microscope or handled glass slides. Introductory lessons and practice sessions using the microscope and related materials will be part of this unit. Frank decides that for these lessons and practice sessions, he will partner students and set up learning stations based on microscope use and safety procedures. He will carefully select student pairs based on a "buddy" system, with one student who is more familiar with these procedures paired with another student who is less familiar.

He also decides that he will have the students work together using a worksheet. On this worksheet, the procedures for using a microscope safely will be outlined step-by-step. Pictures will be used to depict these procedures for Danny, who has severe mental retardation, and for Maria, who has a severe reading disability.

Since Maria responds well to using the computer, Frank decides to have students from one of the middle school technology classes come in before the unit starts and take pictures of a student demonstration of the microscope procedures using the digital video camera. These step-by-step video shorts with accompanying verbal directions will be placed on the computer at one of the learning stations. The still photographs will be used for a classroom chart and for Danny's and Maria's ongoing reference.

Content Modification

Frank will give his students a brief curriculum-based pre-assessment on cells. This assessment will address the objectives he has identified based on the planning pyramid questions. He will also use student learning profiles to identify a number of relevant student characteristics, including interests, learning styles, and abilities. From the results of his data collection, he will begin to modify the content for individual or small groups of students as necessary.

For this unit, however, he plans to provide students with a number of ways to learn and process the content and to demonstrate their understanding. Frank will simplify the content for a number of students by (a) altering the text, (b) providing study guides and practice sheets, and (c) allowing students to use a self-study program with practice exercises on the computer. (Some of these materials have already been developed from the previous years. In addition, Sandra, the special education teacher, said that she would help Frank modify additional materials this year.)

Although Danny will be provided with an alternative curriculum, he will functionally participate with the other students. Danny is interested in science materials and has had experience observing through a telescope and a microscope. (Danny's older brother, who is now in university majoring in chemistry, was in Frank's class five years ago. Danny's brother and parents help to reinforce activities done in school.) Frank will work primarily on objectives from Danny's IEP, including such skills as taking turns, learning the name of his partner and group members as depicted on his picture/symbol communication board, and initiating requests for assistance using the sign for help.

Frank believes that using the microscope and other learning stations in the classroom will help to provide opportunities for Danny to work on his IEP objectives. Danny will not be required to master the cell unit objectives identified for ALL students. Frank will identify several modified objectives for Danny, such as using a microscope safely, distinguishing a plant cell from an animal cell based on color, and placing a label on the nucleus in plant and animal cells depicted in various formats.

The content for Maria and some of the other students will be modified by simplifying the text and the use of study guides, in written text and in a computer text file. The study guide on the computer will be linked to drill and practice exercises. This will be one of the learning centers set up in the room.

Process Modification

Frank plans to use pairs for most activities. However, for some activities, he will use jigsaw groupings. In these groups he will put pairs of students together, making six groups of two pairs each. He plans to use the jigsaw groups to learn new vocabulary words, and to study more about certain topics. For each group, he will ensure that students vary in abilities so that each group will have one student who can explain, demonstrate, and help others with the content or problems.

Frank also plans to provide whole group instruction for short periods of time during each science class. This instruction will include demonstrations at some of the learning stations that will be set up throughout the classroom. For the rest of the science period, pairs of students will work at these stations to perform an activity or activities. Each individual in the pair will have some activities that are the same as the partner's, and some that are different. The stations will provide students with the opportunity to learn and demonstrate understanding using a variety of modes and at varying levels. Frank has set up activities that are tiered at three levels (or more) so all students can participate at their own entry level.

The stations are structured as follows. One station will have materials to construct varying types of cells. Another station will have a computer for viewing information about cells, with varying types of questions to challenge all students at their ability levels. The third station will have a three-dimensional cell that is labeled, and can be taken apart or put together.

The next three stations will have microscopes with prepared slides for viewing cells, accompanied by different types of data recording sheets. The seventh station will have clean slides and materials to make and label new slides for viewing. The eighth station will have a tape-recorder for listening to and taping questions and/or answers for other students. The ninth station will have activities and games to check knowledge and understanding.

The last two stations will be used primarily for research and problem-solving questions/answers. One of the research stations will be in the science classroom and the other will be located in the library. Both of these stations will have computers with Internet access.

Product Modification

As with every unit in the study of life science, students keep a collection of their work assignments in a folder. After the assignments are graded, the students insert them in their work folders. Some students complete their assignments on the computer. Others, like Maria, either tape their assignments or seek assistance from another student in recording the work in a written format.

Danny includes his IEP objectives checklist as well as other assignments that have been recorded for him personally or from group work. Each student's work folder is reviewed with Frank at least once a month, with feedback given.

Educator 3: Geraldo

Geraldo is a high school English teacher who has been teaching for 15 years in an urban school district. He has a master's degree in Educational Administration, and serves as the Chair of the Department of Modern Languages. This department includes composition and literature classes. Spanish and French classes are offered as electives. Geraldo teaches the upper level classes in English literature. His fifth period class is composed of 25 11th graders enrolled in a required course in American Literature. This class is focusing on novels and short stories.

Geraldo has been teaching the 11th grade American Literature courses for 6 years and has had experience prior to this teaching at a middle school. Like Frank in the middle school, he has concerns about trying to teach all the content to all the students. He realizes he must delineate the most important content for student learning so that he can differentiate instruction for students with varying interests, background knowledge and learning profiles.

Geraldo's class consists of 11 boys and 14 girls, ranging in age from 15 to 19 years old. Of these 25 students, there are 2 for whom English is not the primary language, 2 who have been identified as gifted and talented, and 4 who receive special education services. Of those 4 students receiving special education services, Delvin has been identified as having mild mental retardation. Ricky has been diagnosed as having an emotional/behavioral disability. Naomi has been identified as having autism. Wanetta has been diagnosed as having a learning disability.

As Geraldo reviews the Planning Pyramid and the three areas to be considered when using differentiated instruction in a mixed ability classroom, he decides to focus first on the content. The issues that must be addressed are accessibility to the written word, the type of response format to be used, and what should students be able to learn.

Geraldo begins with the three questions of the planning pyramid for his unit on the novel:

1. What will ALL students learn?

2. What will MOST but not all students learn?

3. What will SOME students learn?

In studying the novel, the main concepts to be taught are (a) character, (b) plot, (c) setting, (d) climax, (e) atmosphere, (f) conflict, and (g) theme. Geraldo decides that at the end of this unit ALL students will demonstrate their understanding of character, plot and setting. MOST students will be able to demonstrate their understanding of climax and atmosphere. SOME students will be able to demonstrate their understanding of conflict and theme.

Response Modes

In assessing his class, Geraldo realizes that the diversity of the students in this class will require creative and thoughtful adaptations. For example, two of his students receiving special education services, Naomi and Delvin, and one of his students, Lacina (who speaks English as a second language), will require different modes for obtaining information and for responding.

For example, Naomi does not read, but does comprehend spoken language. She can communicate, and uses about 20 signs. She also has a Dynavox. She uses about 30 symbols although this varies from day to day. Geraldo decides that Naomi will need to have information presented to her visually and auditorially. She will respond in class and on assignments using her augmentative communication systems. Naomi has a teacher aide in class who can help her with various input and response modes. However, Geraldo also wants Naomi to interact more with her peers than with the adults in the classroom. Geraldo believes that with adaptations, Naomi will be able to participate productively in the assigned group activities as well as whole group instruction. He will include several of Naomi's IEP objectives within this unit, such as working with a peer for ten minutes, and using her communication board to initiate a request.

Wanetta and Delvin have specific learning needs that will require adaptations in the mode for inputting information as well as the mode for responding to information and creating a final product. One of Delvin's IEP objectives that Geraldo will address is written productivity. One of

Wanetta's objectives is the use of voice recognition computer software to compose her written work.

With these considerations in mind, Geraldo realizes that other students may be interested in and have a need for using a variety of modes to learn the concepts in this unit. Thinking about the diverse student learning profiles, he feels a bit overwhelmed by the wide differences of student characteristics in this particular class. Geraldo also feels a sense of challenge as he begins to make adaptations to this unit and to various individual lessons.

He realizes that he will have to change his teaching style from primarily lecturing and student readings to other modes that are more visual and tactile. Also, his final product, which in the past has been a written exam demonstrating an understanding of the various concepts of the novel, will need to be changed.

Content Modification

Geraldo will give his students a brief curriculum-based pre-assessment on the novel. This assessment will address the concepts of the novel that he has identified. Geraldo will assess students on all concepts. Then, based on the results of his pre-assessment, he will group students according to the three learning goals he identified from using the Planning Pyramid questions.

Geraldo will also review various student characteristics, particularly student learning styles and interests. Once Geraldo collects this information, he will analyze it and then modify the content for individuals and for groups of students as appropriate. Since Geraldo plans to use various types of instruction and group work activities, he believes that he can incorporate multi-level instruction.

Since Geraldo plans to use two or three American novels for the concepts of study, he would like his students to first "read" one novel together. He has selected The Outsiders by S. E. Hinton. Geraldo will simplify access to the content of this novel for a number of students by allowing them to choose from several formats to "read" The Outsiders.

Most of the students will read the full text of the novel itself. However, Geraldo will develop a number of alternative formats to access the material. These will include various versions of the novel, such as a condensed version, an audio taped version, summary notes (e.g., Cliff Notes), a "comic book" version, and a videotape movie version.

Geraldo will also adapt the content related to the seven concepts that he will be teaching. For example, the first three concepts (character, plot and theme) that ALL students will learn will be defined and presented at three different levels. Geraldo will use a variety of examples from simple to more complex for each of the concepts. For the most simplified level of information for each concept, he will provide a study guide.

Geraldo will also have a learning resource folder for each of the concepts. For the first three concepts, the materials will be simplified. Geraldo will also provide numerous examples from the text for students to use as a reference.

The other four concepts will be presented in similar learning resource folders. Students will be able to use these for initial learning and for reference. The content will be presented in a format that corresponds to three different ability levels. The corresponding activities will consider different student interests and modes of learning. Geraldo plans to have these packets available as part of the multi-level centers on the concepts of the novel.

Process Modification

Geraldo plans to use whole group instruction to introduce the novel, and then to present each concept. While students are continuing their learning at the centers and in paired and small group work activities, he will instruct individual students and small groups of students based on needs.

For example, sometimes Geraldo will use homogeneous "readiness" groupings when students need help to develop the understanding of a concept or to review various components of the novel. At other times, he will establish mixed-readiness groupings when all students can contribute to showing the concept.

For example, as students learn about setting, Geraldo will have students working together in small groups to design a setting of their choice from The Outsiders. Students will create their design using any format such as a diorama, collage, bulletin board, or small stage set. As part of the requirement, each student will contribute to the design of the set they choose. Upon completion, one student from each group will be selected to present their project.

Individual student characteristics and individual student goals will determine the specific mode of communication for the presentation of the project. For example, Delvin may be asked to write three sentences about his group's design. Naomi, with the help of members from her group, may use her Dynavox to present her group's project.

Product Modification

For each concept, Geraldo plans to have a variety of methods for students to demonstrate their understanding. For example, for the concept of "setting," Geraldo may have Naomi use magazines to find pictures to create a setting similar to a room in her home. Delvin may be requested to watch a scene from the movie of The Outsiders. After viewing the scene, he will verbally describe the setting using a tape recorder. From this recording he then will write a description of the scene. Other students may be required to find pictures that represent a setting directly from the novel. Other students may be requested to compare and contrast their home setting to one of the settings in the novel. Some students may research the 1960's, and then describe how the setting reflects this time in American history, particularly for a specific class of people.

For each concept, Geraldo will require "products" that can be developed and presented in a variety of ways, including writing, speaking, making and performing. He will also encourage students to work at various levels of difficulty and involvement depending on their interest in a particular concept.

Summary

Each of the three teachers began the journey by first examining the classroom as it currently existed, the curriculum (explicit, hidden, and absent), the learning profile of the students, and the instructional procedures currently in use. Each teacher then focused on what ALL students should know, what MOST students should know, and what SOME students should know. Each teacher envisioned the different paths that could bring students to the goal. Student readiness, interests, and learning profiles were reflected in the planning process. Flexible grouping, student choice, and modification of content, process, and product are all present. The classroom is rich with profound ideas and relevant to student lives. The journey, while challenging, is made with a joyful appreciation of individual differences. Come join us on this journey.

REFERENCES

Bartlett, L. D., Weisenstein, G. R., & Etscheidt, S. (2002). *Successful inclusion for educational leaders*. Upper Saddle River, NJ: Merrill.

Batzle, J. (1992). *Portfolio assessment and evaluation: Developing and using portfolios in the K-6 classroom*. Cypress, CA: Creative Teaching Press.

Billmeyer, R. & Barton, M. L. (1998). *Teaching reading in the content areas: If not me, then who?* (2nd ed.). Aurora, CO: Mid-continent Regional Educational Laboratory.

Bos, C. S., & Vaughn, S. (2002). *Strategies for teaching students with learning and behavior problems* (5th ed.). Boston: Allyn and Bacon.

Forest, M., & Lusthaus, E. (1998). Promoting educational equity for all students: Circles and MAPS. In S. Stainback, W. Stainback, & M. Forest (Eds.), *Educating all students in the mainstream of regular education* (pp. 43-47). Baltimore: Brookes.

Gardner, H. (1993). *Multiple intelligences: The theory in practice*. New York: Basic Books.

Gardner, H. (1991). *The unschooled mind: How children think and how schools should teach*. New York: Basic Books.

Hoover, J. J., & Patton, J. R. (1997). *Curriculum adaptations for students with learning and behavior problems: Principles and practice* (2nd ed.). Austin, TX: Pro-Ed.

Hourcade, J. J., & Bauwens, J. (2003). *Cooperative teaching: Sharing the schoolhouse* (2nd ed.). Austin, TX: Pro-ed.

Issue: In heterogeneous classrooms, is it feasible to modify instruction to meet students' individual needs-and if so, how? (1994). *ASCD Update Newsletter, 36*(7), 7.

Janney, R. E., & Snell, M. E. (1997). How teachers include students with moderate and severe disabilities in elementary classes: The means and meaning of inclusion. *JASH, 22*(3), 159-169.

Janney, R., & Snell, M. E. (2000). *Teachers' guide to inclusive practices: Modifying schoolwork*. Baltimore: Brookes.

Kaplan, S., Kaplan, J., Madsen, S., & Gould, B. (1980). *Change for children: Ideas and activities for individualizing learning.* Glenview, IL: Scott Foresman.

Kochhar, C. A., West, A., & Taymans, J. M. (2000). *Successful inclusion: Practical strategies for a shared responsibility* (2nd ed.). Upper Saddle River, NJ: Merrill.

Maker, C. J. (Ed.). (1993). *Critical issues in gifted education: Programs for the gifted in regular classrooms* (Vol. III). Austin, TX: Pro-Ed.

Mastropieri, M. A., & Scruggs, T. E. (2000). *The inclusive classroom: Strategies for effective instruction.* Columbus, OH: Merrill.

Mercer, C. D., & Mercer, A. R. (2001). *Teaching students with learning problems* (6th ed.). Upper Saddle River, NJ: Merrill.

Meyen, E. L. (1981). *Developing instructional units for the regular and special teacher* (3rd ed.). Dubuque, IA: Brown.

Miller, S. P. (2002). *Validated practices for teaching students with diverse needs and abilities.* Boston: Allyn and Bacon.

Remus, M. L., & Adcock, B. (1998). *More than shared classrooms: Educating kids with and without disabilities together successfully.* Salt Lake City: The ARC of Utah.

Renzulli, J. S., Leppien, J. H., & Hays, T. S. (2000). *The multiple menu model: A practical guide for developing differentiated curriculum.* Mansfield Center, CT: Creative Learning Press.

Salend, S. J. (2001). *Creating inclusive classrooms: Effective and reflective practices* (4th ed.). Upper Saddle River, NJ: Merrill/Prentice Hall.

Schumm, J. S. (1999). *Adapting reading and math materials for the inclusive classroom.* Reston, VA: Council for Exceptional Children.

Schumm, J. S., Vaughn, S., & Leavell, A. G. (1994). Planning Pyramid: A framework for planning for diverse students' needs during content instruction. *The Reading Teacher, 47,* 608-615.

Shea, T. M., & Bauer, A. M. (1997). *An introduction to special education: A social systems perspective* (2nd ed.). Madison, WI: Brown & Benchmark.

Shore, B. M., Cornell, D. G., Robinson, A., & Ward, V. S. (1991). *Recommended practices in gifted education: A critical analysis.* New York: Teachers College Press.

Tomlinson, C. A. (1995). *How to differentiate instruction in mixed-ability classrooms.* Alexandria, VA: ASCD.

Tomlinson, C. A. (1999). *The differentiated classroom: Responding to the needs of all learners.* Alexandria, VA: ASCD.

Tomlinson, C. A. (2000a). Reconcilable differences: Standards-based teaching and differentiation. *Educational Leadership, 58*(1), 6-11.

Tomlinson, C. A. (2000b). *Differentiating instruction for academic diversity.* Unpublished handout. Boston, MA: ASCD Professional Development Institute.

Tomlinson, C. A. (2001). *Differentiating instruction for academic diversity.* Unpublished manuscript. Boston, MA: ASCD Professional Development Institute.

Tomlinson, C. A., & Allan, S. D. (2000). *Leadership for differentiating schools & classrooms.* Alexandria, VA: ASCD.

Tomlinson, C. A., & Imbeau, M. (1999). Teacher to teacher: Making independent study work. *Teaching for High Potential, 1*(1), 104.

Webber, J. (1997). Responsible inclusion: Key components for success. In P. Zionts (Ed.). *Inclusion strategies for students with learning and behavior problems: Perspectives, experiences, and best practices* (pp. 27-55). Austin, TX: Pro-Ed.

A P P E N D I X

A

Instructional Planning Form

Date: _____ Period: _____ Subject: _____

Goal: _____

Materials Required: _____

	Anticipatory Set	Learning Activity	Rehearsal Activity	Learning Activity	Evaluation Activity
What some will learn:					
What most will learn:					
What all should learn (Goal):					
Adaptations •Content •Product •Process •Environment					

Differentiated Instruction

APPENDIX

B

Websites

http://www.mrddcec.org/

The Division on Developmental Disabilities of the Council for Exceptional Children

http://cec.sped.org/index.html

The Council for Exceptional Children

http://ericec.org

ERIC Clearing House

http://inclusion.com/

Inclusion Press/Inclusion Network; Inclusion Resources

http://www.wall.k12.nj.us/staff_dev/ differentiating_instruction.htm

ASCD's Differentiation Model; ASCD's Strategies; Differentiating Content, Process and Product

http://rushservices.com/Inclusion/homepage.htm

Inclusion...Yours, Mine, Ours

http://tst1160-35.k12.fsu.edu/mainpage.html

Differentiated Instruction (Lessons)

http://web.uvic.ca/~jdurkin/edd401su/Differentiated.html

The Flow of Instruction in the Differentiated Classroom

http://www.allentownsd.org/DifferentiatedInstruction.htm

Allentown School District: Differentiated Instruction Websites and Articles

http://www.readingrockets.org/article.php?ID=154

Helping Kids Who Struggle: Basics of Differentiation

http://www.ascd/org/pdi/demo/diffinstr/differentiated1.html

What is Differentiated Instruction?

http://ascd.org/readingroom/edlead/0009/holloway.html

Research Link—Preparing Teachers for Differentiated Instruction

http://www.circleofinclusion.org/

Circle of Inclusion Home Page

http://www.enhancelearning.ca/differentiating.html

Guidance Learning with Technology—Differentiating Instruction

http://www.twblearn.com/pastconferences/azdi/azcarol_ann_tomlinson.html

Keynote: Teaching in Noah's Ark: Differentiating Instruction in Mixed-Ability Classrooms

http://www.michiganlearning.org/category.asp?CategoryID=6

Partnership for Learning: Differentiated Instruction

http://www.help4teachers.com/

Kathie Nunley's Site for Educators: Layered Curriculum

http://www.edu.gov.mb.ca/ks4/iru/publications/bibliogrpahies/diffin01.html

Multiple Intelligences and Differentiating Instruction: A Bibliography, December 2000

http://www.freeholdtwp.k12.nj.us/Heather%20Web/journey.htm

Journey Toward Differentiation Reading List

http://www.ncrel.org/sdrs/areas/issues/methods/instrctn/in500.htm

Critical Issue: Enhancing Learning Through Multi-Age Grouping

http://www.newhorizons.org/spneeds_intr.html

Inclusive Learning Environment for Students with Special Needs

http://www.people.memphis.edu/~coe_rise/links.html

RISE: Inclusion-Related Links

http://www.sedl.org/change/issues/issues43.html

Inclusion: The Pros and Cons

http://www.niesc.kas.in.us/esc7sdev/mihomepage.htm

Multiple Intelligences Home Page

http://www.teacherswork.com/twshop/differentiated.html

Professional Resources for Educators: Differentiated Instruction

http://www.somers.k12.ny.us/intranet/diffsites.htm

A Sampling of Websites Which Can Help in Differentiating Instruction

http://www.usoe.k12.ut.us/sars/Upi/inclusion_basics.htm

Inclusion Basics

http://www.usoe.k12.ut.us/Upi/curriculum.htm

Curriculum

http://www.weac.org/kids/1998-99/march99/differ2.htm

From Theory to Practice: The Challenges of Heterogeneous Classrooms

http://www.weac.org/kids/1998-99/march99/differ.htm

Teaching in Mixed-Ability Classrooms

Differentiated Instruction